To Mair Rees
with very best wishes,
Helen Dunmore

THE APPLE FALL October 1987

4.99

8/9

Helen Dunmore
THE APPLE FALL

BLOODAXE BOOKS

ISBN: 0 906427 43 6

First published 1983 by
Bloodaxe Books Ltd,
P.O. Box 1SN,
Newcastle upon Tyne NE99 1SN.

Bloodaxe Books Ltd acknowledges
the financial assistance of Northern Arts.

Typesetting & cover printing by
Tyneside Free Press Workshop Ltd, Newcastle upon Tyne.

Printed in Great Britain by
Unwin Brothers Ltd, Old Woking, Surrey.

For my parents

Acknowledgements

Acknowledgements are due to the editors of the following publications in which some of these poems have appeared: *Agenda, Bananas, Delta, Hard Feelings* (Women's Press, 1979), *South West Review, Spare Rib, Stand*, and *Writing Women.*

Helen Dunmore wishes to thank South West Arts for a Writer's Bursary awarded in 1980.

Contents

The marshalling yard

In the goods yard the tracks are unmarked.
Snow lies, the sky is full of it.
Its hush swells in the dark.

Grasped by black ice on black
a massive noise of breathing
fills the tracks;

cold women, ready for departure
smooth their worn skirts
and ice steals through their hands like children
from whose touch they have already been parted.

Now like a summer
the train comes
beating the platform
with its blue wings.

The women stir. They sigh.
Feet slide
warm on a wooden stairway
then a voice calls and
milk drenched with aniseed
drawls on the walk to school.

At last they leave.
Their breathless neighbours
steal from the woods, the barns,
and tender straw
sticks to their palms.

A cow here in the June meadow

A cow here in the June meadow
where clouds pile, tower above tower.

We lie, buried in sunburn,
our picnic a warm
paper of street tastes,

she like a gold cloud
steps, moony.
Her silky rump dips
into the grasses, buffeting
a mass of seed ready to run off in flower.

We stroll under the elder, smell
wine, trace blackfly along its leaf-veins

then burning and yawning we pile
kisses onto the hot upholstery.

Now evening shivers along the water surface.
The cow, suddenly planted, stands—her tender
skin pollened all over –
ready to nudge all night at the cold grasses,
her udder heavily and more heavily swinging.

Annunciation off East Street

The window swings and squeaks in the sun.
Mary says to the angel: 'Come.
My husband is sleepy.
You're rapid and warm-winged.'

First Elizabeth, breathless,
ties up her dates in her heart.
How can a woman be so fortunate?
'Precious baby,' they write on her chart.

Elizabeth the ageing primipara
reminded of her ancestress Sarah
who also slept with an old man.
Bearded, whuffling,
his flesh drew like chicken-skin.

Mary sat with Elizabeth
chopping up parsley, their breath
pregnant, settling the room.
Here Elizabeth crouched for six months
uterus bubbling
while Zacharias snipped the altar flame.

'So it turns out at last.
You fucked with the holy spirit –
I guessed it.
We're both gigantic
at night, feeding our great babies.

I gorge where no-one can see me,
count days, walk tiptoe
still fearing the bloody trickle.'

Mary answered her laughing:
'Elizabeth, let's tell them everything!'

Zelda

At Great Neck one Easter
were Scott
Ring Lardner
and Zelda, who sat
neck high in catalogues like reading cards

her hair in curl for
wild stories, applauded.
A drink, two drinks and a kiss.

Scott and Ring both love her –
gold-headed, sky-high Miss
Alabama. (The lioness
with still eyes and no affectations
doesn't come into this.)

Some visitors said she ought
to do more housework, get herself taught
to cook.
Above all, find some silent occupation
rather than mess up Scott's vocation.

In France her barriers were simplified.
Her husband developed a work ethic:
film actresses; puritan elegance;

tipped eyes spilling material
like fresh Americas. You see
said Scott   they know about work, like me.

You can't beat a writer for justifying adultery.

Zelda
always wanted to be a dancer

she said, writhing
among the gentians that smelled of medicine.

A dancer in a sweat lather is not beautiful.
A dancer's mind can get fixed.

Give me a wooden floor, a practice dress,
a sheet of mirrors and hours of labour

and lie me with my spine to the floor
supple   secure.

She handed these back too
with her gold head and her senses.

She asks for visits. She makes herself hollow
with tears, dropped in the same cup.
Here at the edge of her sensations
there is no chance.

Evening falls on her Montgomery verandah.
No cars come by. Her only visitor
his voice, slender along the telephone wire.

The Polish husband

The traffic halted
and for a moment
the broad green avenue
hung like a wave

while a woman crossing
stopped me and said

'Can you show me my wedding?
—In which church is it going to be held?'

The lorries hooted at her
as she stood there on the island
for her cloak fell back
and under it her legs were bare.
Her hair was dyed blonde
and her sad face deeply tanned.

I asked her 'What is the name of your husband?'
She wasn't sure, but she knew his first name was Joe,
she'd met him in Poland
and this was the time for the wedding.

There was a cathedral behind us
and a sign to the centre of the town.
'I am not an expert on weddings,'
I said, 'but take that honey-coloured building
which squats on its lawns like a cat –
at least there's music playing inside it.'

So she ran with her heels tapping
and the long, narrow folds of her cloak falling apart.
A veil on wire flew from her head,
her white figure ducked in the porch and blew out.

But Joe, the Polish man. In the rush of this town
I can't say whether she even found him
to go up the incense-heavy church beside him
under the bridal weight of her clothes,
or whether he was one of the lorry drivers
to whom her brown, hurrying legs were exposed.

The damson

Where have you gone
small child,
the damson bloom
on your eyes

the still heap
of your flesh
lightly composed
in a grey shawl,

your skull's pulse
stains you,
the veins slip deep.

Two lights burn
at the mouth of the cave
where the air's thin
and the tunnels boom
with your slippery blood.

Your unripe cheeks cling
to the leaves, to the wall,
but your grasp unpeels
and your bruises murmur

while blueness clouds
on the down of your eyes,
your tears erode
and your smile files

through your lips like a soldier
who shoots at the sky
and you flash up in silver;

where are you now
little one,
peeled almond,
damson bloom?

Holiday nights

Rain out on the roof
rain out where the rocks
lie bathed in marine spaciousness

now it's time to draw tighter
as night floods down the telephone wire

shoes slip   clothes drift from their skins
dust falls on glasses of bedside water

almost too sleepy to lift flannel to basin
they stare   eyes dark

the fields are blotted   scents curled
predators stiff on the leaf

the bed gives to the centre   they
sleep   reaching for space

A woman and child sleep

A woman and child sleep in a cottage bedroom,
not stirring, their nightlight
shrouded and evenly burning,

mattresses cover the floor,
the shabby, luminous plaster
draws figures as it has always drawn them,

the child, hot in her red pyjamas,
throws out one cry and goes on sleeping.

Mother coming in at night

My body burns, sleepless,
hearing your quick uneven footsteps –

a pulse rising through water
announces you:
my lovely bubble, your smile.
I grasp but your face is darkness.

Gently you unravel my fingers
and say—What's this? You should be sleeping...

Night air blows from the window
and the glass creaks. You sit lightly.
Your cigarette end dims and brightens.

In love

Mother of a child who sullenly
refuses to feed
while her husband, exhausted,
sleeps without touching her –

mule to the bone
    weightless
    nail-
    biting

I am alone
and wait for you.

Come to me early in the morning
my soul, more than my soul,

over the stone where the sun
lays out its stamens,

don't forget my grey housecoat
quickly open to comfort you.

Poem for Flowenda Brimble

No wonder no new life comes from this
chest tearing bitterness –

each night alone or beside you
I lie silent
my throat aching with tearspit

while you, Flowenda, fat girl
decked in your creaking best dress
stand beside me on the doorstep,

you, my bronze daughter
who burst into the world
without one moment of shame or disappointment,

we have both broken agreements:
you have risen from the grave
and I use an office to write poems.

Sleep in the white grass dear
Flowenda. I laughed at your name.

In Rodmell Garden

It's past nine and breakfast is over.
With morning frost on my hands I cross
the white grass, and go nowhere.

It's icy: domestic. A grain
of coffee burns my tongue. Its heat
folds into the first cigarette.

The garden and air are still.
I am a stone and the world falls from me.

I feel untouchable—a new planet
where life knows it isn't safe to begin.
From silver flakes of ash I shape
a fin and watch it with anguish.

I hear apples rolling above me;
November twigs; a bare existence –

my sister is a marvellous
dolphin, flanking her young.
Her blood flushes her skin

but mine is trapped. Occasional moments
allow me to bathe in their dumb sweetness.

My loose pips ripen. My night subsides
rushing, like the long glide of an owl.

Raw peace. A pale, frost-lit morning.
The black treads of my husband on the lawn
as he goes from the house to the loft
                        laying out apples.

Geology

Hour after hour, the day
lapses, gains,

spread like a seaweed
while the tide rises

pulse over pulse, a heart's
blue shine
then deep, pleasurable water –

I dream of Erasmus and Darwin
in neat helmets, hammering
the ammonites –

the liass tumbles
flaking like fingernails,
the polished
stage of a foetus

slides like a fish and hangs
there by the teeth, a fat
bee in its last week.

Two walkers

Slowly their feet tread up the ridges
where fire sleeps in its furrow,

one flame ripples the ash;
the fire's soft heap
sinks like a closing fist,

here winds blow between wall and roadside;
I lean on a stile and watch the two walkers
as they surmount, decline, making perspectives
soot-fingered on the russety landscape.

The apple fall

In a back garden I'm painting
the outside toilet in shell and antelope.
The big domestic bramley tree
hangs close to me, rosy and leafless.
Sometimes an apple thumps
into the bushes I've spattered with turpentine
while my brush moves with a suck
over the burnt-off door frame.

Towels from the massage parlour
are out on the line next door:
all those bodies sweating into them
each day—the fabric stiffening –
towels bodiless and sex over.

I load the brush with paint again
and I hear myself breathing.
Sun slips off the wall
so the yard is cool
and lumbered with shadows,

and then a cannonade of apples
punches the wall and my arms,
the ripe stripes on their cheeks fall open,
flesh spurts and the juices fizz and glisten.

Two beans

The master of the ship, Antonio,
walked through his brother's fields before he sailed.
The beans were almost ready for harvesting:
he picked a pod and shucked it on his palm.

Two fine beans were dented together,
and without thinking any further
he walked through the maize rows, holding them.

When they were free from the sight of land
Antonio put his hands in his pockets.
His fingers touched on the beans –

he shook them out with impatience
thinking he would feed them to the gulls.
Once again, his hand
curled and did not relinquish them.

Closer to his mind were the countries
from which only water divided him:
their glowing tree lines, their gold
rustle, their profitable strangeness.

Months passed, the beans stuck with him.
Shrivelled and no longer rose-coloured
they stayed within reach of his fingers.

Antonio, still feeling far from home,
watches the fields over his evening wine.
The pods are full again. The maize is ripe.
His brother's children argue over the threshing.

He's still got them, the two beans
that soothed him in another continent.
He asks now why he never planted them.

He leaves his settle and his wine glass
and hurries down the path to the harbour.
There's his unmarked and furrowed acre –
he takes the beans and throws them in the water.

Pictures of a Chinese nursery

Yesterday my stepson came home with school photographs.
The image is altered:
no longer one child
rimmed with a photographer's background
smiling much as he does at home

but three or four placed at a table together
working at egg-boxes, tissue-paper
and friendship enough to shiver their absorbed faces.
'That's Jessica. Sometimes, she gives all of us a kiss.'
Others are pointed out for pissing in school flowerbeds.

On his wall I have stuck a poster of a Chinese nursery.
There is a river, a tree,
a wooden bridge, and far into the distance
thick-packed orchards fruiting and flowering.

On the verandah the children fall into place
as radiant parents stride to the field,

the nursery curls on itself
the day without clocks unfolds
and after dinner their songs fly onto the mountain
as far as the plum orchards where workers stop to eat rice.

Pharaoh's daughter

The slowly moving river in summer
where bulrushes, mallow and water forget-me-not
slip to their still faces.

A child's body
joins their reflections,

his plastic boat
drifts into midstream
and though I lean down to
brown water that smells of peppermint
I can't get at it:
my willow branch flails and pushes the boat outwards.

He smiles quickly
and tells me it doesn't matter;
my feet grip in the mud
and mash blue flowers under them.

Then we go home
masking with summer days the misery
that has haunted a whole summer.

I think once of the Egyptian woman
who drew a baby from the bulrushes
hearing it mew in the damp
odorous growth holding its cradle.

There's nothing here but the boat
caught by its string
and through this shimmering day I struggle
drawn down by the webbed
years, the child's life cradled within.

Domestic poem

So, how decisive a house is:
quilted, a net of blood and green
droops on repeated actions at nightfall.

A bath run through the wall
comforts the older boy sleeping ⌐
meshed in the odours of breath and Calpol

while in the maternity hospital
ancillaries rinse out the blood bottles;

the feel and the spore
of babies' sleep stays here.

Later, some flat-packed plastic
swells to a parachute of oxygen
holding the sick through their downspin,

now I am well enough, I
iron, and place the folded sheets in bags
from which I shall take them, identical,
after the birth of my child.

And now the house closes us,
                    close on us,
like fruit we rest in its warm branches

and though it's time for the child to come
nobody knows it, the night passes

while I sleepwalk the summer heat.

Months shunt me and I bring you
like an old engine hauling the blue
spaces that flash between track and train time.

Mist rises, smelling of petrol's
burnt offerings, new born,

oily and huge, the lorries drum
on Stokes' Croft,

out of the bathroom mirror the sky
is blue and pale as a Chinese mountain.

and I breathe in.

It's time to go now. I take nothing
but breath, thinned.
A blown-out dandelion globe
might choose my laundered body to grow in.

Patrick I

Patrick, I cannot write
such poems for you as a father might
coming upon your smile,

your mouth, half sucking, half sleeping,
your tears shaken from your eyes like sparklers
break up the nightless weeks of your life:

lightheaded, I go to the kitchen
and cook breakfast, aching as you grow hungry.
Mornings are plain as the pages
of books in sedentary schooldays.

If I were eighty and lived next door
hanging my pale chemises on the porch
would I envy or pity my neighbour?

Polished and still as driftwood
she stands smoothing her dahlias;

liquid, leaking,
I cup the baby's head to my shoulder:

the child's a boy and will not share
one day these obstinate, exhausted mornings.

Patrick II

The other babies were more bitter than you
Patrick, with your rare, tentative cry,
your hours of sleep, snuffing the medical air.

Give me time for your contours, your fierce drinking.
Like land that has been parched for half a summer
and smiles, sticky with feeding

I have examined and examined you
at midnight, at two days; I have accompanied you
to the blue world on another floor of the hospital
where half-formed babies open their legs like anemones
and nurses, specialised as astronauts,
operate around the apnoea pillows.

But here you bloomed. You survived,
sticky with nectar. X-rayed, clarified,
you came back, dirty and peaceful.

And now like sunflowers settling their petals
for the last strokes of light in September
your eyes turn to me at 3 a.m.

You meet my stiff, mucousy face
and snort, beating your hand on my breast
as one more feed flows through the darkness, timed
to nothing now but the pull of your mouth.

Weaning

Cool as sleep, the crates ring.
Birds stir and my milk stings me;
you slip my grasp. I never find you
in dreams—only your mouth
not crying
your sleep still pressing on mine.

The carpets shush. The house back silences.
I turn with you, wide-lipped
blue figure

into the underground of babies
and damp mothers fumbling at bras

and the first callus grows on us
weaned from your night smiles.

Clinic day

The midwife whose omniscient hands
drew blood as I draw money out on Tuesdays
calls me to wait. We stand
half off the pavement, she spinning a bicycle pedal,
I rocking a pram.

She will be homeless she says by Friday.
But I can't help her. I want to respond to
her troubles with the sleeping flesh of the baby.
Useless. Her days of him are over.

Here at the clinic they know we are mothers.
I might avert all eyes from the baby,
tie a blue bead to his wrist,
not name him –

yet here they brazenly call him my son,
brandish his name on paper,
tell me how well he gets on.

Breathlessly evil fate stays
by their red door-posts on tiptoe:
they will not play.

Approaches to winter

Now I write off a winter of growth.
First, hands batting the air,
forehead still smeared,

—now, suddenly, he stands there
upright and rounded as a tulip.
The garden sparkles through the windows.

Dark and a heap in my arms;
the thermostat clicking all night.
Out in the road beached cars and winter
so cold five minutes would finish you.

Light fell in its pools
each evening. Tranquilly
it stamped the same circles.

Friends shifted their boots on the step.
Their faces gleamed from their scarves
that the withdrawal of day
brought safety.

Experience so stitched, intimate,
mutes me.
Now I'm desperate for solitude.
The house enrages me.

I go miles, pushing the pram,
thinking about Christina Rossetti's
black dresses—my own absent poems.

I go miles, touching his blankets proudly,
drawing the quilt to his lips.

I write of winter and the approaches to winter.
Air clings to me, rotten Lord Derbies,
patched in their skins, thud down.
The petals of Michaelmas daisies give light.

Now I'm that glimpsed figure for children
occupying doorways and windows;
that breath of succulence
ignored till nightfall.

I go out before the curtains are drawn
and walk close to the windows
which shine secretly.
Bare to the street
red pleats of a lampshade expose
bodies in classic postures, arguing.

Their senseless jokes explode with saliva.
I mop and tousle.

It's three o'clock in the cul-de-sac.
Out of the reach òf traffic,
free from the ply
of bodies glancing and crossing,
the shopping, visiting,
cashing orders at the post office,

I lie on my bed in the sun
drawing down streams of babble.
This room holds me, a dull
round bulb stubbornly
rising year after year in the same place.

The night chemist

In the chemist's at night-time
swathed counters and lights turned down
lean and surround us.

Waiting for our prescriptions
we clock these sounds:
a baby's peaked hush,
hawked breath.

I pay a pound
and pills fall in my curled palms.
Holding their white packages tenderly
patients track back to the pain.

'Why is the man shouting?' Oliver asks me.
I answer, 'He wants to go home.'
Softly, muffled by cloth
the words still come
and the red-streaked drunkard goes past us,
rage scalding us.

I would not dare bring happiness
into the chemist's at night-time.
Its gift-wrapped lack of assistance still presses
as suffering closes the blinded windows.

St Paul's

This evening clouds darken the street quickly,
more and more grey
flows through the yellowing treetops,

traffic flies downhill
roaring and spangled with faces,
full buses
rock past the Sussex Place roundabout.

In Sussex the line of Downs
has no trees to uncover,
no lick of the town's wealth, blue
in smoke, no gold, fugitive dropping.
In villages old England
checks rainfall, sick of itself.

Here there are scraps and flashes:
bellying food smells—last minute buying—
plantain, quarters of ham.
The bread shop lady pulls down
loaves that will make tomorrow's cheap line.

On offer are toothpaste and shoe soles
mended same day for Monday's interview
and a precise network of choices
for old women collecting their pension
on Thursday, already owing the rent man.

Some places are boarded. You lose your expectancy –
soon it appears you never get home. Still
it's a fine on evenings and in October
to settle here. Still the lights splashing look beautiful.

Poem for December 28

My nephews with almond faces
black hair like bunches of grapes

    (the skin stroked and then bruised
    the head buried and caressed)

he takes his son's head in his hands
kisses it   blesses it   leaves it:

the boy with circles under his eyes like damsons
not the blond baby, the stepson.

In the forest stories about the black
father   the jew   the incubus

if there are more curses they fall on us.

Behind the swinging ropes of their isolation
my nephews wait, sucking their sweets.
The hall fills quickly and neatly.

If they keep still as water
    I'll know them.
I look but I can't be certain:

my nephews with heavy eyelids
blowing in the last touches of daylight

my sisters raising them up like torches.

To Maria who lives in shantytown

You can't write poems secretly
through the blue gaps in your eyes.
Write words, write rotting cloth,
US guitars.

The stars loom through the terrace
of roof woven badly together,
your midnight cries are thieved, and verses
torn off like bark from your hands,

so in the city stadiums
long stanzas are unwound;
you are the mash of their paper,
your fingers, your split veins.

Greenham Common

Today is barred with darkness of winter.
In cold tents women protest,
for once unveiled, eyes stinging with smoke.

They stamp round fires in quilted anoraks,
glamourless, they laugh often
and teach themselves to speak eloquently.
Mud and the camp's raw bones
set them before the television camera.

Absent, the women of old photographs
holding the last of their four children,
eyes darkened, hair covered,
bodies waxy as cyclamen;
absent, all these suffering ones.

New voices rip at the throat,
new costumes, metamorphoses.

Soft-skirted, evasive
women were drawn from the ruins,
swirls of ash on them like veils.

History came as a seducer
and said: this is the beauty of women
in bombfall. Dolorous
you curl your skirts over your sleeping children.

Instead they stay at this place
all winter; eat from packets and jars,
keep sensible, don't hunger,
battle each day at the wires.

Poem for hidden women

'Fuck this staring paper and table –
I've just about had enough of it.

I'm going out for some air,'
he says, letting the wind bang up his sheets of poems.

He walks quickly; it's cool,
and rainy sky covers both stars and moon.
Out of the windows come slight
echoes of conversations receding upstairs.

There. He slows down.
A dark side-street—thick bushes—
he doesn't see them.
He smokes. Leaves can stir as they please.

(We clack like jackrabbits from pool to pool of lamplight.
Stretching our lips, we walk exposed
as milk cattle past heaps of rubbish

killed by the edge
of knowledge that trees hide
a face slowly detaching itself
from shadow, and starting to smile.)

The poet goes into the steep alleys
close to the sea, where fish scales line the gutter
and women prostitute themselves to men
as men have described in many poems.

They've said how milky, or bitter
as lemons they find her –
the smell of her hair
...vanilla...cinnamon...
there's a smell for every complexion.

Cavafy tells us he went always
to secret rooms and purer vices;
he wished to dissociate himself
from the hasty unlacings of citizens
fumbling, capsizing –
white
flesh in a mound and kept from sight,

but he doesn't tell us
whether these boys' hair always smelled of cinnamon
or if their nights cost more than spices.

A woman goes into the night café,
chooses a clean
knife and a spoon
and takes up her tray.
Quickly the manageress leans from the counter.
(As when a policeman arrests a friend
her eyes plunge and her voice roughens.)
She points to a notice with her red nail:
'After 11 we serve only accompanied females.'

The woman fumbles her grip
on her bag, and it slips.
Her forces tumble.
People look on as she scrabbles
for money and tampax.
A thousand shadows accompany her
down the stiff lino, through the street lighting.

The poet sits in a harbour bar
where the tables are smooth and solid to lean on.
It's peaceful. Men gaze
for hours at beer and brass glistening.
The sea laps. The door swings.

The poet feels poems
invade him. All day he has been stone-breaking
he says. He would be happier in cafés
in other countries, drinking, watching;

he feels he's a familiar sort of poet
but he's at ease with it.
Besides, he's not actually writing a poem:
there's plenty, he's sure,
in drink and hearing the sea move.

For what is Emily Dickinson doing
back at the house—the home?
A doctor emerges, wiping his face,
and pins a notice on the porch.
After a while you don't even ask.

No history
gets at this picture:
a woman named Sappho
sat in bars by purple water
with her feet crossed at the ankles
and her hair flaming with violets
never smiling when she didn't feel like it.

'End here, it's hopeful,'
says the poet, getting up from the table.

If no revolution come

If no revolution come
star clusters
will brush heavy on the sky

and grapes burst
into the mouths of fifteen
well-fed men,

these honest men
will build them houses like pork palaces
if no revolution come,

short-life dust children
will be crumbling in the sun –
they have to score like this
if no revolution come.

The sadness of people
don't look at it too long:
you're studying for madness
if no revolution come.

If no revolution come
it will be born sleeping,
it will be heavy as baby
playing on mama's bones,

it will be gun-thumping on Sunday
and easy good time
for men who make money,

for men who make money
grow like a roof
so the rubbish of people
can't live underneath.

If no revolution come
star clusters
will drop heavy from the sky

and blood burst
out of the mouths of fifteen
washing women,

and the land-owners will drink us
one body by one:
they have to score like this
if no revolution come.

Tortoise head

I still could easily live
without it I say from years of experience

(but glad to be preoccupied
with flesh as sleet blows on the wall

and to touch babies in clusters
like still air between me and the wind).

I don't forget how easily it happens:
my life tipped on its back,
that scouring, bodily
lack of adjustment –

that moon rising in terror or sadness.

Look. Its jaws lock on a crust.
Raw tortoise—terribly aged but inexperienced
has grown used only to definite occurrences
like lamb's lettuce, and sun in the morning.

A safe light

I hung up the sheets in moonlight,
surprised that it really was so
steady, a quickly moving pencil

flowing onto the stained cotton.
How the valves
in that map
of taut fabric
blew in and blew out

then spread flat
over the tiles
while the moon filled them with light.

A hundred feet above the town
for once the moonscape showed nothing extraordinary

only the clicking pegs
and radio news from our kitchen.
One moth hesitated
tapping at our lighted window

and in the same way the moonlight
covered the streets, all night.

Near Dawlish

Her fast asleep face turns from me,
the oil on her eyelids gleams
and the shadow of a removed moustache
darkens the curve of her mouth,

her lips are still flattened together
and years occupy her face,
her holiday embroidery glistens,
her fingers quiver then rest.

I perch in my pink dress
sleepiness fanning my cheeks,
not lurching, not touching
as the train leaps.

Mother, you should not be sleeping.
Look how dirty my face is, and lick
the smuts off me with your salt spit.

Golden corn rocks to the window
as the train jerks. Your narrowing body leaves me
frightened, too frightened to cry for you.

The last day of the exhausted month

The last day of the exhausted month
of August. Hydrangeas
purple and white like flesh immersed in water
with no shine
to keep the air off them
open their tepid petals more and more widely.

The newly-poured tar smells antiseptic
like sheets moulding on feverish skin:
surfaces of bedrock, glasslike passivity.

The last day of the exhausted month
goes quickly. A brown parcel
arrives with clothes left at the summer lodgings,
split and too small.
A dog noses
better not look at it too closely
God knows why they bothered to send them at all.

A smell of cat
joins us just before eating.

The cat is dead but its brown
smell still seeps from my tub of roses.

Harvest festival

Rain stands off, this still morning.
Gary and Matthew bring sheaves
of stick beans out of the allotment,

Lisa comes running, late,
with two sprays of Michaelmas daisies.
I put them in the green jar
next to yesterday's branch of fuchsia.

Strange how precise and exotic they are
close to –
I pass a dozen dun-coloured gardens
walking to school.

The separate red lines of housing trail
over the hill
at the end of the day two children
dragging a pram
look in the hedges for privet-moth caterpillar.

Close, they gaze at its stripes,
their pale heads similar, down-looking,

and frown, touching its back gently
as they have sometimes touched the fuchsia petals.

Sunlight at Christmas

Once there were dips among the pollened
bone shadows,
once her hair hissed
under the nightly sweep of the brush.
Each morning she pinned it,
eyes sticky, not lighting the candle.

She was that kind of easy, fair girl,
then she got married.

Twenty, pregnant again,
she rose early.
She pulled the blinds and sunlight splashed
close on her damp petticoat.

Sleepy one day and left alone
I sniffed the ruching on her pink bodices,

the skin that touched me was soft
the veins on her cheeks made roses.

Under her dresses words
whispered above me
hushing like winds
amidst the carving of lamb.

'Mother' they said, 'Don't stand.'
Shoes hurt her now; she wears slippers
all day and suffers in town.
Timid, she leans to the shop mirrors.

Here by the sunlit Christmas display
our bodies pack us. Her ghost waits,
quick, in a shop-girl's uniform,
making the best of ponderous women.

Second marriages

These second marriages arching within
smiles of their former friends:
his former wife and her child-swapping
remnants of weekday companionship,
her former husband, his regular
friends who encircled her
those wet Saturdays after the baby was born.

The children's early birthdays, the tea
and talk about socialization;
the shared potties.
Frozen in these is the father's
morning exit from the maternity hospital.

Sliced from the album those gowns
that blood; the shawl in a heap,
those marital triumphant
glances at night when they got him to sleep.

Second marriages endure without these
public and early successes,
no longer tempting others or fate
by their caresses.

The deserted table

Coiled peel goes soft on the deserted table
where faïence, bubble glasses, and the rest
of riches thicken.

People have left their bread and potatoes.
Each evening baskets
of broken dinner hit the disposal unit.

Four children, product of two marriages,
two wives, countless slighter relations
and friends all come to the table

bringing new wines discovered on holiday,
fresh thirtyish faces, the chopped
Japanese dip of perfectly nourished hairstyles,
more children, more confident voices,
wave after wave consuming the table.

The writer's son

The father is a writer; the son
(almost incapable of speech)
explores him.

'Why did you take my language
my childhood
my body all sand?

why did you gather my movements
waves pouncing
eyes steering me till I crumbled?

We're riveted. I'm in the house
hung up with verbiage like nets.
A patchwork monster at the desk
bending the keys of your electric typewriters.

You're best at talking. I know
your hesitant, plain vowels.
Your boy's voice, blurred,
passed through my cot bars, stealing my baby magic.
You were the one they smiled at.'

Ollie and Charles at St Andrew's Park

Up at the park once more
the afternoon ends.
My sister and I huddle in quilted jackets.

A cigarette burn
crinkles the pushchair waterproofs,
the baby relaxes
sucking his hood's curled edges.

Still out of breath
from shoving and easing the wheels
on broken pavement we stay here.
Daffodils break in the wintry bushes

and Ollie and Charles in drab parkas
run, letting us wait by the swings.
Under eskimo hoods their hair springs
dun coloured, child-smelling.

They squat, and we speak quietly,
occasionally scanning the indigo patched
shadows with children melted against them.

Winter fairs

The winter fairs are all over.
The smells of coffee and naphtha
thin and are quite gone.

An orange tossed in the air
hung like a wonder
everyone would catch once,

the children's excitable cheeks
and woollen caps that they wore
tight, up to the ears,
are all quietened, disbudded;

now am I walking the streets
noting a bit of gold paper? –
a curl of peel suggesting the whole
aromatic globe in the air.

Melting snow

I pass the barracks　　　the stone
pitted　　　the cherry tree broken

I pass a yellow-faced man
with one French loaf in his pocket
I am ignored
he calls his voice gulldiving.

In gutters snow water rushes
wheels smash

diesel uncrystallises　　　pumps
dab　　　traffic flows onward
sailing into white anaesthesia.

One with a paraffin can
stays lapped in the slush.
Time slips to the past:

I lose you lolling on my knee
your kid scalp glistening

for I'm uncovering
the thaw
walks by the river Aura,
children fat-legged in padded trousers.

Ice creaks and I trail homewards
stiffly across the linked islands

passing the barracks, the Finnish
soldier's scarcely stirring
coat hem.

In a wood near Turku

The summer cabins are padlocked.
Their smell of sandshoes
evaporates over the lake water
leaving pine walls to shoulder the ice.

Resin seals them in hard splashes.
The woodman
knocks at their sapless branches.

He gets sweet puffballs
and chanterelles in his jacket,
strips off fungus like yellow leather,
thumbs it, then hacks the tree trunk.

Hazy and cold as summer dawn
the day goes on,

wood rustles on wood,
close, as the mist thins
like smoke around the top of the pine trees
and once more the saw whines.

Roman villa

Nailbrush of pale wood like the table
scoured into a hollow,
the sea outside swallowing
breath after breath.

I walked with my mother along the shore
hearing the grey waves on one side of me
brim and then topple

and in the mornings I heard
summer voices calling from inside to outside.
A too-white landscape butted the window.

I see the builder's sign nearby,
the JCB, the plain
marks of a future habitation.
Now buddleia draws bees to its foundations

and classroom murmurs
try to crack open the poem.

Under a white, tender
October sky I file
peering at tessellations

stuck at this unreadable pavement.
And now we come to the fourth Georgic:
ox, beaten to jelly, humming with bees.

The ox falls with its nostrils stoppered.
The pavement in the Roman holiday house
offers it smiling faces
while the workman, following directions,
shuffles his digger backwards.

Landscape from the Monet Exhibition at Cardiff

My train halts in the snowfilled station.
Gauges tick and then cease
on ice as the track settles
and iron-bound rolling stock creaks.

Two work-people
walk up alongside us,
wool-wadded, shifting their picks,

the sun, small as a rose,
buds there in the distance.
The gangs throw handfuls of salt like sowers
and light fires to keep the points moving.

Here are trees, made with two strokes.
A lady with a tray of white teacups
walks lifting steam from window to window.

I'd like to pull down the sash and stay
here in the blue where it's still work time.
The hills smell cold and are far away
at standstill, where lamps bloom.

Breakfast

Often when the bread tin is empty
and there's no more money for the fire
I think of you, and the breakfast you laid for me
—black bread and honey and beer.

I threw out a panful of wine yesterday –
the aluminium had turned it sour –
I have two colours of bread to choose from,
I'd take the white if I were poor,

so indigence is distant as my hands
stiff in unheated washing water,
but you, with your generous gift of butter
and cheese with poppy seeds, all in one morning meal

have drawn the blinds up at the bedside window
and I can watch the ships' tall masts appear.

Helen Dunmore was born in 1952 in Beverley, Yorkshire. She studied English at York University, and after graduating in 1973 lived in Finland for two years. Married with a stepson and a son, she now lives in Bristol, and has just finished training as a nursery teacher.

Helen Dunmore's poems have appeared in many magazines. *The Apple Fall* is her first collection.

Pete Henry was born in 1943 in Kingston-upon-Thames and served his time as a hand engraver in London from 1959 to 1964. In 1976 he founded Aquila Engraving in Newcastle, and has since worked extensively for print, particularly intaglio and relief processes. His work has been shown at the Royal Academy and at the Royal Society of Painter Etchers.